COPTIC ORTHODOX
PATRIARCHATE

See of St. Mark

THE NATURE OF CHRIST

BY
H.H. POPE SHENOUDA III

Title	: The Nature of Christ
Author	: H. H. Pope Shenouda Ill
Illustrated by	: Sister Sawsan
Edition	: 1st Print, Ottowa, 1985
	2nd Print Cairo, Oct. 1991
Typesetting	: J.C.Center
Press	: Dar El-Tebaa El-Kawmia
Legal Deposit No	: 7005/1991.
Revised	:COEPA -1997

H.H. Pope Shenouda III
117th Pope and Patriarch of Alexandria
and the See of St Mark

INTRODUCTION

The nature of Christ is a very important subject that caused a serious dissension within the Church in the fifth century, in 451 AD. When the theological dialogue started as an effort towards the unity of churches, the subject had to be discussed. Therefore, our Orthodox Church found it necessary to issue a book which presents its concept in this regard in a language fit for theological dialogues.

This subject (the Nature of Christ) was taught by me to the students of the Seminary "St. Mark Theological College" in 1984 in the form of lectures which I delivered to them in St. Bishoy Monastery, Sheheit Desert, as part of the courses of comparative Theology. The lectures were printed merely for the use of the students.

The same lectures were afterwards translated into English in Ottawa, Canada, in 1980 and became available in English only for six years...

We had to print them in Arabic for the students of the Seminary and its branches and for the benefit of those who are interested in theological studies whether ministers or ordinary individuals.. and whoever has the desire-from other churches to be acquainted with our concept of Christology.

The first theological dialogue we attended on this subject was in Vienna, Austria in September 1971 AD convened by the Pro-Oriente Group. In this dialogue we reached a theological formula that was accepted by our Catholic brothers and those in the old Oriental orthodox churches: the Syrians, Arminians, Ethiopians and Indians. It was an important dialogue indeed, for the dissension that occurred in the fifth century had distorted the face of every church before the other.. But now the way is open for a common understanding.

Then, there was an official agreement with the Catholic churches after 17 years of differences (since 1988), based on the previous understanding. The agreement was recorded in a concise "Statement" which you will find at the end of this book.

There was another dialogue, in more detail, with our brothers in the Byzantine Orthodox Churches in St. Bishoy Monastery, Sheheit Desert in 1989 AD It was attended by the theologians of twenty Orthodox Churches and was followed by another meeting of the priestly representatives of the Orthodox churches in Chambesy, Geneva, in 1990.

Now, seeing it is necessary to make our people acquainted with the details and evidences that prove our concept of the Nature of Christ,

And since the Pro-Oriente Group is convening a religious conference for the representatives of all Churches at the end of October 1991 to present to them the Agreed Statement on Christology.

And since we were asked to present a paper on the subject and deliver it as a lecture in the conference.

Therefore, we proceeded to print the former lectures delivered in the Seminary in 1984 as a book to be presented to the conference and to be available in Arabic and in English for all who are interested.

Pope Shenouda III

THE ORTHODOX CONCEPT REGARDING THE NATURE OF CHRIST

The Lord Jesus Christ is God Himself, the Incarnate Logos. Who took to Himself a perfect manhood. His Divine nature is one with his human nature yet without mingling, confusion or alteration; a complete Hypostatic Union. Words are inadequate to describe this union. It was said, that without controversy, *"Great is the mystery of godliness: God was manifested in the flesh, (1 Tim. 3:16).*

As this union is permanent, never divided nor separated, we say in the liturgy that His Godhead never departed from His manhood for a single moment nor even for a twinkle of an eye.

The Divine nature (God the Word) was united with the human nature which He took of the Virgin Mary by the action of the Holy Spirit. The Holy Spirit purified and sanctified the Virgin's womb so that the Child to whom she gave birth would inherit nothing of the original sin; the flesh formed of her blood was united with the Only-Begotten Son. This unity took place from the first moment of the Holy Pregnancy in the Virgin's womb.

As a result of the unity of both natures-the Divine and the human-inside the Virgin's womb, one nature was formed out of both: "The One Nature of God the Incarnate Logos" as St. Cyril called it.

The Holy Church did not find an expression more reliable, deep and precise than that which was used by St. Cyril the Great, and which St. Athanasius the Apostolic used before him. Both of them were true leaders in the theological field worldwide.

When I participated in the dialogue arranged by the ProOriente group in Vienna, Austria in September 1971 between the Roman Catholic Church and the ancient Oriental Orthodox Churches concerning the Nature of Christ, the point of discussion was St. Cyril's expression "One Nature of God the Incarnate Logos" (Mia Physis Tou Theou Logou Sesarkwmene).

After the schism which took place in the year 451 AD, when the Coptic Orthodox Church rejected the motions of the Council of Chalcedon and its theological struggles, we were called "Monophysites" that is, those who believe in the "One Nature".

Sharing our belief are the Syrians, the Armenians, the Ethiopians and the Indians; who were also called "NonChalcedonian" Orthodox Churches.

On the other hand, the Chalcedonian Catholic and Greek Churches "The Roman Orthodox" believe in the two natures of Christ; the Protestant Churches also hold this belief.

Consequently, these churches are known as "Diophysites" - believers in the two natures of Christ.

The Roman - or Chalcedonian - Orthodox Churches include those of Constantinople, Greece, Cyprus, Russia, Romania, Hungary and Serbia as well as the Roman Orthodox Churches of Egypt, Syria, Lebanon, America and the St. Catherine Monastery in the Sinai desert.

The term "Monophysites" used for the believers in the One Nature has been intentionally or unintentionally misinterpreted throughout certain periods of history. Consequently, the Coptic and the Syrian Churches in particular were cruelly persecuted because of their belief, especially during the period which started from the Council of Chalcedon held in 451 AD and continued to the conquest of the Arabs in Egypt and Syria (about 641 AD).

This misinterpretation continued along history as though we believed in one nature of Christ and denied the other nature.

We wonder which of the two natures the Church of Alexandria denies?

Is it the Divine nature? Certainly not, for our Church was the most fervent defender against the Arian heresy in the Council of Nicea, held in the year 325 AD, as well as before and after that. Or is it The Lord's human nature that the Church of Alexandria denies? St. Athanasius of Alexandria resolved this entirely in the oldest and greatest book on this subject **The Incarnation of the Word,**

The expression "One Nature" does not indicate the Divine nature alone nor the human nature alone, but it indicates the unity of both natures into One Nature which is "The Nature of the Incarnate Logos".

The same applies when we speak about our human nature which comprises two united natures: the soul and the body. Thus, man's nature is not the soul alone nor the body alone, but their union in one nature called human nature. We will discuss this point in detail later.

St. Cyril the Great taught us not to talk about two natures after their unity.

So we can say that the Divine nature united hypostatically with the human nature within the Virgin's womb, but after this unity we do not ever speak again about two natures of Christ. In fact, the expression "two natures" implies in itself division or separation, and although those who believe in "the two natures" admit unity, the tone of separation was obvious in the Council of Chalcedon - a matter which prompted us to reject the Council and caused the exile of St. Dioscorus of Alexandria.

Before we go further in explaining the subject of the One Natures and the two natures of Christ, we would like to give a brief description of the widely known heresies concerning the Nature of Christ.

[2]

WIDELY KNOWN HERESIES
CONCERNING THE NATURE OF CHRIST

A) The Heresy of Arius (Arianism):

Arius denied the Divinity of the Lord Jesus Christ; he considered that Christ was not consubstantial with the Father and that He was created.

The roots of Arianism still exist until this day. Even after being condemned in 325 AD by the Council of Nicea, Arius and his followers caused trouble, dissension and suspicions within the Holy Church.

B) The Heresy of Apollinarius:

Apollinarius preached the Divine Nature of Christ, but did not believe in His complete human nature; he considered that the human nature of Christ was not in need of a soul and thus He was without soul because God the Logos provided the needed life. As this implied that the human nature of Christ was incomplete, the Holy Ecumenical Council of Constantinople held in 381 AD condemned Apollnarius and rejected his idea declaring it a heresy.

C) The Heresy of Nestorus (Nestorianism):

Nestorus was Patriarch of Constantinople in 428 AD, he was excommunicated by the Holy Ecumenical Council of Ephesus held in 431 AD because he refused to name the Virgin St. Mary

"Mother of God" (Theotokos). He believed that St. Mary gave birth to a mere human and that Divinity descended and filled this human; Thus the Virgin Mary would be called the "Mother of Jesus" (Christokos), and not the "Mother of God" (Theotokos).

Nestorus priest, Anastasius, spread this teaching; and Nestorus then confirmed it and wrote five books to refute the idea that the Virgin was the "Mother of God".

In so doing he is considered to have denied the Divinity of Christ.

His theory that Divinity descended and filled Our Lord meant that there was no Hypostatic union, but rather meant that the Divinity descended to accompany Him or to fill Him as in the case of saints.

In other words, Nestorus' concept meant that Christ became a dwelling for God just as He became a dwelling for the Holy Spirit through His Baptism. As such, Christ is considered a "Carrier of God" (Theophorus), which is the same title given to St. Ignatius of Antioch.

He Explained that it was impossible for the Virgin to give birth to God, as the creation never gives birth to the Creator. Besides, whatever is born of flesh will merely be flesh.

Thus the opinion of Nestorus was that the relation between the human nature of Christ and the Divine nature started just after His Birth from the Virgin and it was not a Hypostatic union. He explicitly said: "I distinguish between the two natures". **In this way the Nestorian belief is against the Propitiation Creed,** because if Christ has not united with the Divine nature it would have been impossible for Him to offer an unlimited propitiation (or sacrifice) sufficient for the forgiveness of all sins of all people throughout the ages.

When our Church says that the Virgin is the "Mother of God", it confirms that she gave birth to the Incarnate Logos and not that she was the source of the Divine nature. Certainly not.

God the Logos is the Creator of the Virgin, but He, in the fullness of time, descended and filled her and she became pregnant and carried Him united with the human nature and she gave birth to Him.

The twelve Anathemas which St. Cyril issued include answers to all the Nestorian heresies. He condemned those who said that the two natures resulted from being joined together and those who said that God the Logos was working in the man Jesus or that God the Logos was dwelling in Jesus. He also condemned those who distinguished between Jesus and God the Logos claiming that He was merely a man born of a woman.

D) The Heresy of Eutyches (Eutychianism):

Eutyches was an archimandrite of a monastery in Constantinople. **He zealously opposed the Nestorian heresy, and was so highly concerned about the unity of the two natures in Christ, which Nestorus tore apart, that he fell into another heresy.**

Eutyches said that the human nature was absorbed and dissolved in the Divine nature as a drop of vinegar in the ocean. In this way, he denied the human nature of Christ.

After St. Dioscorus had excommunicated him, Eutyches pretended that he repented and accepted the true faith and St. Dioscorus allowed him to return on the condition that he would refute his heresy. Later on however, he again declared his corrupt belief and was condemned by the Council of Chalcedon held in 451 AD, and was also excommunicated by the Coptic Church.

The Council of Chaicedon:

In spite of the fact that the Council of Ephesus had excommunicated Nestorus, the Nestorian roots extended to influence the council of Chalcedon where the trend to separate the two natures became so apparent that it was said that Christ is two persons, a God and a human being; the one works miracles and the other accepts insults and humiliation.

Following the same trend, Leo, the Bishop of Rome, accordingly declared his famous Tome which was rejected by the Coptic Church. But the Council accepted and voted for it, thus confirming that two natures existed in Christ after their unity: a Divine nature performing its functions and a human nature carrying out its role.

Nestorus claimed that those two natures were distinctly separate. The Carthage's Council proclaimed their union but Nestorus separated them by this explanation. Just as he concluded that Christ had two natures, he also concluded that He had two wills and two lines of action.

The problem of the two natures and two wills has its roots here and thus began disruption and conflict within the Church. Now we are trying to settle this question by attempting to rewrite a satisfactory wording of our faith, which would be acceptable to all.

[3]

THE NATURE OF THIS UNION

Union Without Mingling, Confusion, Alteration or Transmutation:

By "one Nature", we mean a real union. This does not involve mingling as of wheat and barely, nor confusion as of wine and water or milk and tea. Moreover, no change occurred as in the case of chemical reaction. For example carbon dioxide consists of carbon and oxygen, and the nature of both changes when they are combined; each loses its properties which distinguished it before the unity. In contrast, no change occurred in the Divine or Human nature as a result of their unity.

Furthermore, unity between the two natures occurred without transmutation.

Thus, neither did the Divine nature transmute to the human nature, nor did the human nature, transmute to the Divine nature. The Divine nature did not mix with the human nature nor mingle with it, but it was a unity that led to Oneness of Nature.

THE EXAMPLE OF THE UNION
BETWEEN IRON AND FIRE

St. Cyril the Great used this analogy and so did St. Dioscorus. In the case of ignited iron, we do not say that there are two natures: iron and fire, but we say iron united with fire. Similarly, we speak about the nature of the Lord Jesus Christ, the Incarnate God, and we do not say "God and man".

In the union of iron with fire, the iron is not changed into fire nor fire into iron.

Both are united without mingling, confusion or alteration. Although this situation is not permanent in the case of iron, and here is the point of disagreement, but we only want to say that once iron is ignited with fire, it continues to retain all the properties of iron and all the properties of fire.

Likewise, the nature of the Incarnate Logos is One Nature, having all the Divine characteristics and all the human as well.

THE EXAMPLE OF THE UNION
BETWEEN THE SOUL AND THE BODY

This example was used by St. Cyril, St. Augustine and a large number of ancient and recent theologians.

In this simile, the nature of the soul unites with the physical earthly nature of the body to form a union of one nature, which is the human nature.

This united nature does not include the body alone nor the soul alone but both together are combined without mixing, confusion, alteration or transmutation. No transmutation occurs of the soul into the body nor of the body into the soul, yet both become one in essence and in nature, so we say that this is one nature and one person.

Hence, if we accept the idea of the unity between the soul and the body in one nature, why do we not accept the unity of the Divine and the human into one Nature?!

Here we'd like to raise an important question regarding the One Nature and the Two Natures:

Do we not all admit that the nature which we call Human Natures contained before the unity two Natures: the soul and the body? yet, those who claim that there are two natures in Christ: a divine and a human, do not mention the two natures of manhood i.e. the soul and the body but consider them one.

If we go into details we would find ourselves before three natures in Christ!!! the Divinity, the soul and the body, and each of them has its distinct entity and essence... Of course, this is unacceptable on both sides.

When we accept the union of the soul and the body in one nature in Christ, and when we use the expression theologically, it becomes easier for us to use the expression "One Nature of Christ" or "One Nature of God, the Incarnate Logos".

Just as we say that the human nature is one nature consisting of two elements or natures, we can also say about the Incarnate Logos, that He is one entity of two elements or natures.

If the Divine nature is claimed to differ from the human nature, how then do they unite? The reply is that the nature of the soul is fundamentally different from the nature of the body, yet it is united with it in one nature, which is the human nature.

Although man is formed of these two natures, we never say that He is two, but one person. All man's acts are attributed to this one nature and not to the soul alone or to the body alone. Thus when we want to say that a certain individual ate, or became hungry, or slept, or felt pain, we do not say that it is his body which ate, or became hungry, or got tired or slept or felt pain. All man's acts are attributed to him as a whole and not only to his body.

Similarly, all the acts of Christ were attributed to Him as a whole and not to His Divine nature alone (independently) or to His human nature alone.

This was explained by Leo in the Council of Chalcedon and we shall give further explanation to this point later on, God willing.

The union of the soul and body is an intrinsic real union, **a Hypostatic one. So is the union of the Divine nature of Christ with the human nature in the Virgin's womb. It is a Hypostatic union, self-essential and real and not a mere connection, then separation as Nestorus claimed.**

Though the example of the union of the soul and body in the human nature is inclusive, still it is incomplete as it does not explain how the soul departs the body by death nor how they reunite again in the resurrection.

But as for the unity of the Divine and human natures of Christ, it is an inseparable union as the Divine nature never departed the human nature for one single moment nor for a twinkle of an eye.

[4]

THE UNITY OF NATURE AND THE
BIRTH OF CHRIST

To whom did the Virgin give Birth? Did she give birth to the Godhead only? Did she give birth to the manhood only? Did she give birth to God and man? or did she give birth to the Incarnate God?

It is impossible to say that she gave birth to God alone, because she gave birth to a Child who was seen by everybody, nor that she gave birth to man only (or a pure human nature), otherwise we revert to the heresy of Nestorus.

What does the Bible mean by saying, *"The Holy Spirit will come upon you, and the power of the Highest will overshadow you; therefore, also, that Holy One who is to be born will be called the Son of God. " (Luke. 1:35)*? Again, what is the meaning of the verse stating that the Son shall be named Emmanuel which is interpreted *"God with us. " (Matt. 1:23)*? And what is the meaning of Isaiah's words: *"For unto us a Child is born, Unto us a Son is given; And the government will be upon His shoulder. And His name will be called Wonderful, Counselor, Mighty God, Everlasting Father, Prince of Peace." (Is 9: 6)*. Therefore, He (Christ) is not just a man, but the Son of God, Emmanuel and the Mighty God.

The Virgin did not give birth to a man and God, otherwise she would be said to have had two sons: one being God and the other, man. We are thus left with the evidence that she gave birth to the "Incarnate God."

Christ is not two Sons, one the Son of God to be adored, and the other a man and not to he worshipped.

We can not separate between the Divine and the human nature of Christ. As stated by St. Athanasius the Apostolic regarding the Lord Jesus Christ, he is not binatured, to one we kneel down and to the other we do not, but He is rather of One Nature - the Incarnate Logos - that is one with His Body and before whom we kneel down in one genuflection.

Therefore, our worship is not offered to the Divine nature apart from the human nature. There is no separation and consequently, all worship is to the Incarnate God.

The Lord Jesus is the Only-Begotten Son, Who was born from the essence of the Father before all ages." *For whom He foreknew, He also predestined to be conformed to the image of His Son, that He might be the firstborn among many brethren."(Rom.8:29).* According to one of the fathers, He was born from the Father before all ages without a mother, and was born from a Virgin in the fullness of time without an earthly father.

Hence St. Paul the Apostle said: *"But when the fullness of the time had come, God sent forth His Son, born of a woman, born under the law" (Gal 4:4).*

Therefore, He who was born of the Virgin was the Son of God and at the same time the Son of Man as He used to call Himself.

The Son (the Logos) filled the womb of the Holy Virgin, took from her His human nature and then she delivered Him. This differs from what Nestorus claimed that the Virgin gave birth to an ordinary man and that later on, God dwelt in this man or filled Him or that Christ just became a Theophorus (a carrier of God) without a Hypostatic union.

For this reason we worship this born Child and say to Him in the Trisagion hymn: "Holy is God, Holy is the Almighty, Holy is the Everliving, who was born of the Virgin, have mercy upon us". This conforms with the words of the holy angel who told the Virgin: "The Holy One born of you is called the Son of God".

In Christ, the Divine nature was united with the human nature in the womb of the Virgin. That is why when the Virgin visited Elizabeth, the blessed old woman said to her:
"But why is this granted to me, that the mother of my Lord should come to me? " (Luke. 1:43).

At that time St. Mary was still pregnant and yet, was entitled "The Mother of God".

The Creed states: "We believe in one God, Jesus Christ, the Only-Begotten Son (of God), who was born before all ages... who for us (we human beings) and for our salvation descended from heaven and was conceived of the Holy Spirit and of the Virgin Mary, became Man and was crucified for our sake. He suffered, was buried and rose......

Therefore, this Only-Begotten Son is the same One who descended from Heaven and was Incarnated. He is God Himself who descended into the Virgin's womb and was incarnated.

This opposes Nestorus' claim that he was Originally man and that God dwelt in Him after His Birth! The One Who was Incarnated was originally the Only-Begotten Son of God born before all ages.

Thus He was able to say to the Jews while speaking to them, *"Before Abraham was, I am. " (John. 8:58).* He did not say, "My Divine nature existed even before Abraham", but He said, "I am", which proves the unity and Oneness of His Nature.

[5]

POSSIBILITY OF SUCH UNITY

This unity between the Divine nature and the human nature is possible, otherwise it would not have been fulfilled, it was known to God ever since the world began: He has preconceived and planned it through His fore - knowledge of what man needed for his salvation. For this reason St. Paul the Apostle said about the Incarnation of the Lord Jesus: *"According to the revelation of the mystery kept secret since the world ..but now is made manifest. (Rom. 16:25).*

There is also a contemplation by one of the fathers on the verse *"Eye has not seen, nor ear heard, Nor have entered into the heart of man The things which God has prepared for those who love Him." (1 Cor. 2:9)*, which refers to eternal happiness; that father said the things that had not entered into the heart of man were the Incarnation of God (becoming man), His crucifixion and His death for our sake in order to redeem and purchase us with His precious Blood.

Another father said that the presence of God among His creation takes 3 forms: either general existence due to His being present everywhere, or through His Grace bestowed On His Saints, while the third unique form which happened only once, is His consubstantiality with Christ when the Divine nature united with the human nature in the Virgin's womb.

The One Nature of the incarnate Logos:

It is One Nature (one entity) but has all the properties of two natures:

It has all the properties of the Divine nature and all those of the human nature. In this One Nature, the. body was not transmuted to the Divine nature but remained as a body, the body of God the Logos. The Logos, also was not transmuted to be a human nature but remained as it is the Divine nature though united with a body. His Divine nature is not susceptible to death while His human nature is liable to die. Both the Divine and the human natures united in essence in the Hypostasis and in nature without separation.

No separation occurred between the Divine nature and the human nature at Christ's death:

As we say in the Syrian Fraction, concerning the death of Christ "The soul left the body but His Divinity never departed neitherfrom His Soul nor from His Body. His Soul likewise, whilst united with His Godhead, descended into hell to preach those who died in the faith and to open to them the gates of Paradise and let them enter. Yet His Body, also united with His Godhead, remained in the grave. "

On the third day His soul, united with His Godhead, came to unite with His body which was also united with His Godhead; Thus resurrection took place.

Consequently, the Incarnate God risen from the dead **was capable of coming out of the tomb while it was closed and sealed by a huge stone.** It was also possible for the One Lord to **enter through the closed doors and meet with His disciples** *(John. 20:19).*

Did He enter through the closed doors by His Divine nature or by His human nature? Is not this an evidence of the One Nature? and which one came out of the tomb? was it the Divine nature, the human nature, or Christ the Incarnate Logos?

We are not dealing here with two natures: God and a man, for this expression signifies two and not one, and the term "Two" does not ever denote unity.

A Union, actually, cannot be separated into two.

I would like to use the term "union" to talk about what happened in the Virgin's womb, but at the next stage we call it "One Nature". Similarly, the term "Two" denotes separation or the liability to separate.

[6]

THE IMPORTANCE OF THE "ONE NATURE" FOR PROPITIATION AND REDEMPTION

The belief in the One Nature of the Incarnate Logos **is essential, necessary and fundamental for redemption**. Redemption requires unlimited propitiation sufficient for the forgiveness of the unlimited sins of all the people through all ages. There was no solution other than the Incarnation of God the Logos to offer this through His Divine Power.

Thus, if we mention two natures and say that the human nature alone performed the act of redemption, it would have been entirely impossible to achieve unlimited propitiation for man's salvation. Hence comes the danger of speaking of two natures, each having its own specific tasks.

In such case, the death of the human nature alone is insufficient.

Accordingly St. Paul Says:
" For had they known, they would not have crucified the Lord of glory. " (1 Cor. 2:8).

He did not say; they would not have crucified the man Jesus Christ. The term *"Lord of Glory"* here affirms the One Nature and its necessity for redemption, propitiation and salvation; this is because the one who was crucified is the Lord of Glory. Obviously, He was crucified in the body, but the body was united with the Divinity in One Nature, this is the essential basis for salvation.

St. Peter says to the Jews: ".*But you denied the Holy One and the Just, and asked for murderer to be granted unto you **and killed the Prince of Life.** " (Acts 3:14,15)*. Here he confirms that the One crucified was the *"Prince of Life"* a term which denotes divinity. St. Peter never separated the 'two natures or facts involved in the crucifixion, due to the importance of their unity for the enactment of redemption.

St. Paul also says in his letter to the Hebrews: *"For it was fitting for Him, for whom are all things and by whom are all things, in bringing many sons to glory, **to make the captain of their salvation perfect through sufferings" (Heb. 2:10)***

Whilst suffering, He never forgot His divine message: *"For by Him were all things created. " (Col. 1:16)*. In another instance St. Paul says: *"For Him and by Him all things"*.

When the Lord Jesus Christ appeared to St. John the Visionary, He said to him:
"I am the First and the Last, *I am He that lives, and was dead and behold, I am alive for evermore Amen... and have the Keys of hell and death." (Rev. 1:1 7,18)*.

Thus it is He Who was dead that is the First and the Last and in Whose Hands are the keys of hell and death.

Here Christ did not separate His Divine nature from His human nature while speaking about His death.

Therefore, He who died is the Lord of Glory, the Prince of life, the Prince of Salvation and the First and the Last.

It is very dangerous, for our salvation, to separate between the two natures. Perhaps some would say 'who declared such separation? Is it not the Council of Chalcedon that declared the belief in two united natures?! Yes, it did but the Tome of Leo says also that Christ is two: God and man, the One astonished us with miracles and the other received disgrace and suffering!

What then? If that one being is alone the receiver of suffering, then where is the salvation we gained?!

[7]
THE ONE NATURE AND
THE SUFFERING

Surely, Divinity is not susceptible to suffering, but when the human nature underwent suffering, it was united with the divine nature. Thus pain was inflicted upon this one Nature.

This Explains why the Creed set by the Holy Council of Nicea says, *"The Only-Begotten Son of God descended from heaven, was Incarnate and became man and was crucified for our sake in the reign of Pilate, suffered and was buried and rose from the dead".*

There is a great difference between saying that the human nature alone, apart from the Divine nature, suffered, and that the Incarnate Only-Begotten Son was crucified, suffered, was buried and rose from the dead. Thus, here we find the advantage of believing in the One Nature which provides effective unlimited redemption.

But, did the Divinity suffer?

We say that, essentially, the Divine nature is not susceptible to suffering yet He suffered due to His humanity, and was physically crucified. Hence we say in the prayer of the None (the sixth hour), "You who have tasted death physically in the sixth hour".

He, the man, united with the Godhead, physically died and His death provided unlimited atonement.

The holy fathers explained this point through the aforementioned clear example of the red-hot iron, it is the analogy equated for the Divine Nature which became united with the human nature. They explained that when the blacksmith strikes the red-hot iron, the hammer is actually striking both the iron and the fire united with it. The iron alone bends (suffers) whilst the fire is untouched though it bends with the iron.

As for the crucifixion of Christ, the Holy Bible presents us with a very beautiful verse; St. Paul the Apostle speaks to the bishops of Ephesus asking them: *"... to shepherd the church of God which He purchased with His own Blood." (Acts 20:28);* he ascribes, the Blood to God, although God is Spirit, and the Blood is that of His human nature.

This expression is the most wonderful proof of the One Nature of the Incarnate Logos; what is related to the human aspect can be attributed to the Divine nature at the same time without distinction, as there is no separation between the two natures.

The separation between the two natures claimed by Nestorus failed to provide a solution to the question of propitiation and redemption. The Coptic Church insisted on the expression of the One Nature due to the importance of this matter and to its consequences.

We often say "Mr. X died" but we do not say that his body alone died, seeing that the spirit is in the image of God, and God has bestowed on it the blessing of immortality.

If the first aim of the Incarnation is redemption, and redemption cannot be fulfilled through the human nature alone, faith in the One Nature of the Incarnate Logos is an essential and undeniable matter. Redemption cannot be fulfilled if we say that the human nature alone underwent suffering, crucifixion, blood-shedding and death. Turn to the Holy Bible and read what it says about God the Father,

"He who did not spare His own Son, but delivered Him up for us all, how shall He not with Him also freely give us all things? " (Rom. 8:32) and also,

*"For God so loved the world that **He gave His only begotten Son**, that whoever believes in Him should not perish but have everlasting life. " (John. 3:16), and "In this is love, not that we loved God, but that He loved us and sent His Son to be the propitiation for our sins." (1 John. 4:10).*

Thus, the One sacrificed by God is the Son, the Only Begotten Son, that is, the Second Hypostasis (Person) of the Holy Trinity; the Logos. The Bible did not say that He sacrificed His humanity or anything of the kind although He died on the cross with His human body, this is clear proof of the One Nature of God the Logos, and herein is the importance of this unity for the act of redemption.

The Bible also says in this context, *"God the Father Who has delivered us from the power of darkness and has transferred us **into the kingdom of His Dear Son, in Whom we have redemption through His blood, even the forgiveness of sins**, Who is the Image of the Invisible God." (Col. 1:13-15).*

When the Bible speaks about the forgiveness of sins through the Blood of Christ, it attributes this to the Son Who is the Image of the Invisible God, and to Whom is the kingdom. This is more evidence of the One Nature and the concern of the Holy Bible dealing with the matter of redemption.

Another Similar example is apparent in the parable mentioned by Christ about the wicked vinedressers. He says:

"But when the vinedressers saw the son,....So they took Him and cast Him out of the vineyard and killed Him. " (Matt. 21:37-39).

Here, death is attributed to the Son, and He did not specify His human body. How profound are these words concerning the One Nature".

The Holy Bible proves to us the One Nature of Christ by attributing to the Incarnate Word all acts and qualities that some attribute to one of the two natures, and we shall start by quoting the verses which throw light on the Son of Man.

[8]

THE TERM "SON OF MAN"

The Use of the Term "Son of Man" Where Reference is to the Divinity:

No doubt, the term "Son of Man" denotes the human nature of Christ just as the phrase "Son of God" denotes His Divinity.

However, our Lord Jesus Christ used the term "Son of Man" on several occasions where He meant "Son of God" of which I mention a few:

(1) He explained that the Son of Man is in heaven and on earth.

He told Nicodemus *"No one has ascended to heaven but He who came down from heaven, that is, the Son of Man who is in heaven." (John. 3:13).*

So who is that Son of Man who descended from heaven? And who is he that is in heaven and speaks to Nicodemus on earth? Is it the Divine nature or the human nature? He cannot be the Incarnate Logos. Therefore, this statement very clearly indicates the One Nature.

(2) The Lord Jesus Christ said, *"For the Son of Man is Lord even of the Sabbath day". (Matt. 12:8)*

If the expression "Son of Man" means (or denotes) the human nature, and "the Lord of the Sabbath" denotes the divine nature, then being put together in one statement is another proof of the One Nature.

(3) He said, that the Son of Man has power on earth to forgive sins *(Matt. 9:6).*

But no one forgives sins except God alone. So was the one who said to the paralized man "Your sins are forgiven" the human nature or the Divine one? Is it not preferable to say that it is the Incarnate Logos?

(4) The Lord Jesus Christ says that the Son of Man is the One Who shall Judge the world.

So is it the human nature that will judge the world or the Divine nature? He also says: *"For the Son of Man will come in the glory of His Father with His angels, and then He will reward each according to his works. " (Matt. 16:27).* We notice here that:

He says the "Son of Man " and at the same time "in the glory of His Father".

That is: He defines "Son of Man" and "Son of God" in one statement, indicating the One Nature. Further He Says: "The Son, of Man with His angels", while the words "His angels" indicate His Divine nature.

Thus, we notice here that the term "Son of Man" cannot indicate the human nature alone nor the Divine Nature alone, but indicates the unity of the two natures or the One Nature of the Incarnate Logos.

(5) We find the previous term *in (Matt. 25:31-34):*

"When the Son of Man shall come in His glory and all the holy angels with Him, then He will sit upon the throne of His Glory.. and He will set the sheep on His right hand, but the goats on the left. Then the King will say to those on His right hand come you blessed of My Father, inherit the Kingdom prepared for you from the foundation of the world".

Here the "Son of Man " and "Father" are used in one phrase.

This means that the speaker is the Son of Man and the Son of God at the same time. *"For the Father judges no one, but has committed all judgment to the Son" (John. 5:22).* And here the unity of natures (the One Nature) is obvious.

(6) The Lord Jesus Christ said to the high priest during His trial,

"Hereafter you will see the Son of Man sitting on the right hand of power, and coming in the clouds of heaven. " (Matt. 26:63-65). In this context, St. Stephen said at the time of his martyrdom: *"Look I see the heavens opened and the Son of Man standing on the right. hand of God?" (Acts 7:57).*

So, who is the One sitting on the right hand of power and coming in the clouds of heavens? Is He the One with the human nature or the one with the Divine nature?

It is impossible to separate here but we can say that it is the One Nature, the Nature of the Incarnate Logos.

(7) The Son of Man calls the Angels "His angels" and the elect "His elect".

He says, *"And He (the Son of Man) will send His angels with great sound of a trumpet, and they shall gather together His elect.." (Matt. 24:29-31).*

Here, as the "Son of Man", He acts as God, we cannot explain this phrase by saying that in one instance it is the human nature and in the other it is the Divine nature. For the speaker is the Lord Jesus the Son of Virgin Mary, as well as the Son of God, the Judge of the whole world, Who has supreme power over the angels and can send them, and has power over human beings and can collect His elect from the extremities of the heavens. It is One Nature which cannot be split or severed into two.

(8) Our Lord Jesus Christ, talking to His disciples said,

What, and if you. will see the Son of Man ascend up where He was before. " (John 6:62). What is important here is the phrase "Where He was before", meaning that he was in heaven at first. Obviously He Who was in heaven is the Son "Hypostasis". But here, due to the One Nature, He says concerning the Son of Man what He says about the "Hypostasis" of the Son because He is the Incarnate Word.

This is consistent with what He said to Nicodemus about the Son of Man, that is it *"He that came down from heaven."(John. 3:13),* while He that came down from heaven is the Son "hypostasis", meaning the Divine nature.

In the same sense, St. Paul says about the Lord Jesus Christ that He is the *"Lord from heaven."*
 (1 Cor. 15:47).

[See my book "So Many Years With the Problems of the People (part ll.)" for more details about this point concerning the Son of Man.]

EVIDENCES -FROM THE BIBLE

Several Verses in the Holy Bible Prove the One Nature:

(1)   God the Father Himself testified for Jesus Who was baptized by John the Baptist saying, *"This is My Beloved Son in whom I am well pleased. " (Matt. 3:17).*

Certainly, He did not say this about the human nature of His Son, as His human nature is inseparable from His Divine nature. This verse cannot indicate two, it refers to one, and here it indicates the One Nature of the Incarnate Word.

(2) John the Baptist gave the same testimony when he pointed at Christ and said: *"This is the One of Whom I spoke.* ***He that comes after me is preferred before me for He way before me. " (John 1:15,30).***

So how could He have been before him and come after him? Our Lord came after John the Baptist by human birth and was before him by the Divine nature.

The Baptist did not separate between the human nature and the Divine nature, as he said, "This who came after me (the Incarnate Logos) Was before me". Here the One Nature is obvious, for the One Who John baptized was He Himself who was before him.

(3) St. John The Evangelist says in his Gospel *"No one has seen God at any time.* ***The only begotten Son, who is in the***

bosom of the Father, He has declared Him. " (John. 1:18). The Only-Begotten Son is God the Logos, and the Second Hypostasis. How then did He declare the Father? Certainly when He became Incarnate. Can we say then that the One who declared this was the human nature? St. John Says about Him: "The Only-Begotten Son Who is in the bosom of the Father, He has declared" while we know that it is the Man Jesus Christ who declared Him, and this indicates the One Nature.

(4) The same words are spoken by the same apostle in his first epistle, *"That which was from the beginning, which we have heard, which we have seen with our eyes, which we have looked upon, and our hands have handled, concerning the Word of life" (1 John. 1:1).* He talks about Him Whom he has seen and touched, as the One Who was from the beginning, that is, God. So how did they see God and touch him unless He was the Incarnate logos? These words are not about the human nature alone, nor about the Divine nature alone because the human nature was not eternal from the beginning and the Divine nature alone cannot be touched.

(5) The same meaning is conveyed in the conversation between our Lord Jesus Christ and the man who was born blind. When the Lord opened his eyes, the man asked Jesus ***"Who is the Son of God"*** *and the Lord told him "you have seen Him and **it is He that talks with you. " (John. 9:35-37).***

The Son of God is God the Logos incarnate, that is, the Divine nature. But who was speaking with the blind man, was it merely the human nature? It cannot be the human nature alone because the Lord Jesus Christ confirms that "*it is He that talks with you, the Son of God. " Thus He is the Incarnate God Who was manifest in the flesh (1 Tim. 3:16).*

(6) St. Paul the Apostle says about the Jews when they were in the desert of Sinai, *"and all drank the same spiritual drink.* ***For they drank of that spiritual Rock that followed them, and that Rock was Christ" (1 Cor. 10:4).***

It is well known that those Jews were in the desert of Sinai fourteen centuries before the birth of Christ, so how could He be with them quenching their thirst unless St. Paul is speaking about the Divine nature which is God the Logos? Yet God the Logos was not called Christ until the time of His Incarnation. But due to the One Nature the Apostle Could not distinguish and spoke about the eternity of Christ and His presence before His Birth.

The Apostle proceeds in the same manner: *"nor let us tempt Christ, as some of them also tempted, and were destroyed by serpents" (1 Cor. 10:9).*

(7) Before whom did the Wisemen fall down and worship *(Matt. 2:11)*? Did they worship the Divine nature alone? No, they fell down and worshipped a Child in a manger and they presented unto Him gifts. Did they worship the human nature? The human nature cannot be worshipped.

Thus the only answer left is that they worshipped the Incarnate God just as the man born blind did later, and as those who were in the ship did, when the Lord rebuked the wind and walked on the water; They did not worship Him merely out of respect for *"Those who were in the boat came*

and worshipped Him, saying, 'Truly You are the Son of God."
(Matt. 14:23).

(8) We also ask who it was who walked on the sea water and
rebuked the wind, was it the Divine or the human nature?
There is no doubt that He was the Incarnate Logos.

**The same applies to all the other miracles of Christ; Who
worked those miracles? Was it the Divine nature alone?**

Then what is the meaning of the Phrase *"and He laid His hands
on every one of them and healed them. (Luke. 4:40)*? and
what can we understand from the healing of the woman, who
had a flow of blood and it dried up when she touched His
clothes *(Mark. 5:29)*? In opening the eyes of the blind, who
was it who spat on the ground and made clay of the spittle and
anointed the eyes of the blind with the clay.

No doubt it was He Who performed all those miracles and
several similar ones, **the Lord Jesus Christ, the Incarnate
Logos.** St. John, the Evangelist, says *"**And truly Jesus did
many other signs in the presence of His disciples**, which are
not written in this book" (John. 20:30).* Notice here the use of
the name (Jesus).

We shall be satisfied with presenting the above examples,
because if we follow closely the Holy Bible we may indulge in
an endless process, as the verses referring to the One nature are
extensively used throughout. For this reason we shift now from
discussing the One Nature to a related subject, ie. "the One
Will".

[10]

THE ONE WILL AND THE ONE ACT

Has the Lord Christ two wills and two actions, that is a Divine will and a human will, as well as two actions, that is, a divine act and a human act? As we believe in the One Nature of the Incarnate Logos, as St. Cyril the Great called it, likewise:

We believe in One Will and One Act:

Naturally, as long as we consider that this Nature is One, the Will and the Act must also each be one.

What the Divine nature Chooses is undoubtedly the same as that chosen by the human Nature because there is not any contradiction or conflict whatever between the will and the action of both.

The Lord Jesus Christ said: *"My meat is to do the Will of Him that sent Me to finish His work. " (John. 4:34)*. This proves that His Will is the same as that of the Father. In this context, He said about Himself *" the Son can do nothing of Himself, but what He sees the Father do; for whatever He does, the Son also does in like manner." (John. 5:19)*.

He does not seek for Himself a will that is independent of that of the Father. Consequently He Says *"For I have come down from heaven, not to do My own will, but the will of Him who sent Me. " (John 6:38)*.

It is obvious that the Father and the Son in the Holy Trinity have One Will, for the Lord Jesus Christ said: *"I and My Father are One. " (John. 10:30).*

Hence, since He is one with Him in the Godhead, then He is essentially one with Him concerning the Will. Again, the Son, in His Incarnation on earth, was fulfilling the Will of the heavenly Father. Thus it must be that He Who united with the manhood had One Will.

In fact, Sin is nothing but a conflict between man's will and God's.

But remember that our Lord Jesus Christ had no sin at all. He challenged the Jews saying: *"Which of you convicts Me of Sin?. " (John. 8:46).* Therefore, His Will was that of the Father.

The Saints who are perfect in their behaviour achieve complete agreement between their will and the Will of God, so that their will becomes that of God, and the Will of God becomes their will.

And St. Paul the Apostle said *"But we have the mind of Christ. " (1 Cor. 2:16).* He did not say that our thoughts are in accord with the mind of Christ, but that "we have the mind of Christ", and here the unity is stressed.

If this is said about those with whom and in whom God works, then how much more the unity between the Son and His Own manhood would be in all that is related to the will, the mind and the power to act! He, in Whom the Divine nature has united with the human nature, a Hypostatic and Essential union without separation-not for a second nor a twinkle of an eye.

If there was not unity between the Will of the Divine nature of Christ and His human nature, this would have resulted in internal conflict. Far be it from Him! How then could Christ be our guide and our example... to follow in His footsteps *(1 John. 2:6)?*.

The complete righteousness which marked the life of our Lord Jesus was due to His Divine as well as His Human will. The same is true of the salvation of mankind, the message for which Christ came and said: *"For the Son of Man has come to save that which was." (Matt. 18:11).* This is the same Will of the Father who *"He loved us and sent His Son to be the propitiation for our sins. " (1 John. 4:10).* Thus, the crucifixion was the choice of the Divine as well as the human nature. Had it not been One Will, it would not have been said that Christ died by His Own Will for our sake.

Since the Will is One, the Act is necessarily One.

Here we do not distinguish between the two natures.

AGREED STATEMENT ON

CHRISTOLOGY

"We believe that our Lord, God and Saviour Jesus Christ, the Incarnate - Logos is perfect in His Divinity and perfect in His Humanity. He made His humanity One with His Divinity without Mixture, nor Mingling, nor Confusion. His Divinity was not separated from His Humanity even for a moment or twinkling of an eye.

At the same time, we anathematize the Doctrines of both Nestorius and Eutyches".

Signatures.

CONTENTS